GETTING STARTED

From The Moving Toward Maturity Series

Barry St. Clair

For information
write Reach Out
Youth Solutions at:
info@reach-out.org
Visit our website at:
www.reach-out.org

An Encouraging Word

Now that you have received Jesus into your life, you have entered into an amazing adventure that will affect your life positively, now and forever.

As you get started, what is God's desire for your life? The Apostle Paul described it well: "So then, just as you received Christ Jesus as Lord, continue to live in Him, rooted and built up in Him, strengthened in the faith as you were taught, and overflowing with thankfulness." My prayers go with you as you pursue getting started in the great adventure of knowing Jesus.

PLEASE NOTE: To make *Getting Started* simple and consistent, the pronoun "he" is used throughout rather than "she" or "he/she". In no way is this intended to slight women!

Special Thanks

To Bill Jones, Keith Naylor, and Chris Frear, who worked with me on this project.

To those special people who allowed me to learn the truths of this book on them.

To Kim Doud and Ralph Rowland who graciously allowed me to use the concept and some of the contents of their material *Plugging into God* © 1982 by the Light and Power Co. Used by permission. All rights reserved.

What's Ahead

Uses For This Book

On Your Own. You can go through this book by yourself. If you do, tell at least one other person what you discover.

One-on-One. You can meet with the friend who led you to Christ, getting together at least once a week to grow together.

Group Study. You can use this book with a group. The group should meet six different times. You can meet more than once a week if you like.

Practical Hints

 How to get the most out of this book:
 ➤ Begin each session with prayer.
  Ask God to speak to you. Pray for each other's needs.

 ➤ Use a Bible.
  Try the New International Version or the New Living Bible.

 ➤ Work through the sessions.
  Look up the Bible verses.
  Think through the answers.
  Write the answers.
  Jot down any questions that come up.
  Memorize the assigned verse.

 ➤ Apply each Bible study to your life.
  Act on what you are learning. Obey God in your relationships, attitudes, and actions.
  Talk over these issues with other believers who can encourage and advise you.

G E T T I N G   S T A R T E D   S E S S I O N   1

What Happened When I Accepted Christ?

What person do you most enjoy being around? Why are you so close to that person? Because you like each other and know each other well. The better you know and like someone, the more comfortable you feel with him or her. But you had to meet that person and then spend time together in order to get to know each other.

When you received Jesus Christ, you met Him for the first time. Now you have the privilege of getting to know Him. The more time you spend with Him, just like with any other person, the better you will know Him and the more comfortable you will feel around Him. You want to gain confidence in your new relationship with Jesus.

The first step in getting to know Jesus better is to understand your relationship. As you answer the important questions below, write down what you think happened to you when you accepted Jesus.

What did Jesus Christ do for you when you accepted Him?

_____

How are you different now that you have received Christ?

_____

How can you have confidence that Jesus lives in your life?

_____

How do you feel about that?

_____

Now let's see how God answers these questions in the Bible. Before you read the answers provided, write what you discover in your own words.

What did Jesus Christ do for you when you accepted Him? Read John 1:12.

_____

When you asked Jesus to come into your life, you became a child of God. You can experience a close relationship with God that only a child of God can have. But your relationship with God is even closer than a father/child relationship because Jesus actually lives inside of you. You have His constant companionship.

What makes you different from a person who has not accepted Christ?
Read 2 Corinthians 5:17.

_____

The moment you accepted Christ you became an entirely new person. You might look, feel and even act like you used to, but the Bible says you are completely new and different. Your old selfish desires and attitudes are being replaced by new Christ-like desires and attitudes. What are some of the changes that you see in your life already? (This is a good question to ask yourself every week.)

How can you be sure that Jesus is in your life? Read 1 John 5:11-13.

Since you accepted Jesus, you have the Son and you have life. You can be confident of that because God has promised. Your confidence is not in yourself, but in Jesus Christ.

How important are your feelings? Read John 10:27-30.

You have started the most exciting adventure a person can experience — a personal relationship with Jesus. He wants you to know Him and to enjoy Him. He will guide you, protect you, and help you to grow in your relationships. Your only responsibilities are to

7

PRAYER TIP:

Prayer is simply talking to God. Don't worry about saying the "perfect" words. He is more concerned with your attitude than with your words.

spend time with Him, to trust Him, and to obey Him. You may feel excited, or you may not feel any different. Either way, don't worry.

Feelings are tricky. Your feelings will go up and down. But your faith is based on facts. So rather than rely on your feelings, you must rely on the facts in the promises of the Bible. No matter how you feel, Christ always remains faithful to you.

Right now, thank Jesus for what He has done for you and for your new relationship with Him.

 Summarize your prayer here:

_____

_____

 MOVING OUT

→ > Read back over all of your answers and write down any questions you want to ask.

_____

_____

_____

8

➤ List the three most important areas of your life (parents, studies, friends, sports, etc.) Describe how your new relationship with Christ will make a difference in each area.

1. _____

_____

_____

2. _____

_____

_____

3. _____

_____

_____

He who has the Son has life; he who does not have the Son of God does not have life.

Memory Verse: 1 John 5:12

How Do I Communicate With God?

Your physical growth accelerates at your age more than any other time in your life. In the same way that your physical growth accelerates, your spiritual growth can speed up as well. How can you grow? You will grow by learning to communicate with God. That means learning how to listen to and talk to God.

Listen to Jesus

Jesus wants to communicate with you. He sent the Holy Spirit to live inside you so you can hear what He has to say. What will God say to you through the Holy Spirit?

➤ John 14:15-17 _____

➤ John 14:26 _____

➤ John 16:13 _____

God wants you to hear from Him through the Bible. What is the value of listening to God through reading the Bible? Read Psalm 1:1-3.

_____

_____

As you begin to read the Bible daily and apply what it teaches, your life will change. Follow these simple guidelines for reading the Bible.

➠ ⟩ Pray and ask the Holy Spirit to help you understand the Bible and apply it.

➠ ⟩ Read one chapter a day in a modern translation. Begin by reading through the Book of Mark.

➠ ⟩ Select what you think is the most important verse in the chapter and write it out in your own words.

Talk to Jesus
You can talk to Jesus at any time and in any place. But to have an intimate conversation, it is important to have time alone. You can tell Jesus how you feel, and what you think. Since God knows what is going on in your mind and heart anyway, you can be completely honest with Him.

What clues for talking with God can you find in the following verses?

➠ ⟩ Mark 1:35 _____

➠ ⟩ John 15:7 _____

➠ ⟩ Philippians 4:6-7 _____

➠ ⟩ 1 John 5:14-15 _____

As you pray daily you will learn to communicate with God. Follow this simple outline to help you talk to God in a meaningful way.

> **To Help You Communicate**
> A special notebook will help you in your communication with Jesus. You can order the *Time Alone with God Notebook* from Reach Out Youth Solutions.
> • **www.reach-out.org**

Record the days you meet with God this week.

☐ Sunday ☐ Thursday
☐ Monday ☐ Friday
☐ Tuesday ☐ Saturday
☐ Wednesday

I write these things to you who believe in the name of the Son of God so that you may know that you have eternal life. This is the assurance we have in approaching God: that if we ask anything according to his will, he hears us.

**Memory Verse:
1 John 5:13-14**

Praise Tell God one of His character qualities that you like. Read a Psalm.

Confession Admit your sins to God. Be honest. Then claim His promise of forgiveness in 1 John 1:9.

Thanksgiving Make a list of several things you are thankful for.

Petition Ask God for what you need. He desires to give you what you need.

Intercession Pray for other people. Begin with your family and friends.

These "ways to pray" will help you know what God is saying to you and what you are saying to Him. Write down your thoughts as you go through these "ways to pray" every day. (The *Time Alone with God Notebook* will help you learn more about this.)

MOVING OUT

➤ Decide on a time to read the Bible and pray each day. Find a time when you can be alone with God.

Time: _____

➤ Decide on a place where you will not get interrupted.

Place: _____

➤ Go to: **www.reach-out.org** to order the *Time Alone with God Notebook*

GETTING STARTED SESSION 3

How Do I Tell Other People?

Sometimes the person you are the closest to is the hardest one to tell something significant and meaningful. Usually that's because you desperately want that person to understand and you are afraid he won't. Communicating openly and positively, especially with your parents and friends, is the best way to go. Yet not all parents and friends will respond the same way.

Check the statement that best represents your parents' and friends' response to your new relationship with Jesus, or what you think it might be.

Parents **Friends**

❑ ❑ *"We're excited for you!"*

❑ ❑ *"It's your life."*

❑ ❑ *"We don't understand."*

❑ ❑ *"That's the most ridiculous thing we've ever heard."*

No matter how your parents and friends respond to your decision to follow Jesus, you need to love them and obey Jesus. Practically, how can you do both?

What Do I Tell My Parents?
On a scale of 1-10, rate your relationship with your parents:

Very Bad   1   2   3   4   5   6   7   8   9   10   **Very Good**

Regardless of the quality of your relationship, your parents are very important people in your life. Since your new relationship with Jesus will change your life, your parents need to know about your decision to follow Jesus. What is the best approach to communicate that properly?

Recognize your parents' authority over you. How can you respond properly to your parents, even if they oppose your decision to follow Christ? What will be the results?

 Read Ephesians 6:1-3. _____

_____

Communicate with your parents. Openly talk to your parents about what Jesus means to you, but never argue or force your belief in Jesus on them. How can you do that?

 Read Ephesians 4:15. _____

_____

Earn your parents' trust. Live like a Christian at home by loving your parents and obeying them completely. Then they will trust you and see the positive effect of your relationship with Jesus. How can you do that?

 Read Ephesians 5:29-32. _____

_____

Recognize your parents' needs. Instead of thinking about your own needs, look for ways to meet your parents' needs.

Read Philippians 2:3-4? _____

_____

Your parents will watch you closely to see if your decision to follow Jesus is just another "phase" you are going through or something real and lasting. Don't be a "one-week wonder." Let them see that Christ's presence in your life is permanent. Don't try to be perfect, just obey Jesus and be lovingly honest with your parents.

What Do I Tell My Friends?
Think about your three best friends. What do you think each person's response will be when you tell them about your new relationship with Jesus?

Name   Response

_____   _____

_____   _____

_____   _____

Your friends are likely to have one of three reactions to you receiving Jesus Christ.

Defend

The defenders say something like, "Hey, Jesus may be fine for you, but I'm not so bad. I don't need that." The followers of Jesus encountered the same response. How did Philip's friend, Nathanael, defend himself when he encountered Jesus? **Read John 1:43-49.**

How did Philip overcome Nathanael's defensiveness? Philip didn't try to argue or force Nathanael to do anything he didn't want to do. He simply invited Nathanael to "come and see." Jesus took over from there. You can use the same response with your defensive friends. Instead of arguing, invite them to take a serious look at Jesus Christ.

Desert

You can expect some of your friends to desert you because they think you have become a "weirdo Jesus freak." They react that way because of fear, guilt, "religious" hypocrites, past experiences, or closed minds. You may feel rejected by your friends. Even Jesus was rejected. Hundreds of years before Jesus was born, the Prophet Isaiah wrote how Jesus would be treated. What happened when He was rejected? **Read Isaiah 53:3-5.**

How did Jesus respond when people rejected Him? **Read 1 Peter 2:23.**

Even though your friends may not want to talk about Jesus, love them, pray for them, and keep on talking to them. Live to please Jesus, not your friends. Who knows? In time they could change their minds and come to Jesus.

Decide

For every person who defends his lifestyle or deserts you, many others will say something like, "I've had a lot of thoughts and questions about Jesus. Can we talk about it some more?" Many of your friends want to know more about God, but just don't know who to ask. The following suggestions will help you know how to talk to your friends.

Don't be a people pleaser. The Apostle Paul describes the conflict between trying to please your friends and pleasing God. **Read Galatians 1:10.** Explain it in your own words.

_____

Live to please Jesus, yet still spend time with your friends. What will happen if you do both of these? **Read 1 Thessalonians 1:5.**

_____

Love your friends. How much should you love them? **Read John 15:12.**

_____

Rely on the Holy Spirit to reach your friends. What will be the result when you do?

Power Thought

No matter how your parents respond, God can use their response to help you grow.

. . . .

 Read 1 Corinthians 2:4-5.

 Boldly communicate the message of Jesus to your friends. Even though the Holy Spirit convinces your friends to follow Jesus, God wants to use you to present the Gospel to them. How does God do that? **Read Romans 1:16.**

No one has more potential to reach your friends than you. Ask God to use you to help your friends know Him.

 MOVING OUT

– > Write down how you want to tell your parents about your relationship with Christ.

– > Pray for and plan a time to talk to your parents about your decision to follow Jesus. When?

Power Tip

Verbally identify with Jesus Christ when you are with your friends. Say out loud "I belong to Jesus Christ."

➤ List the one major attitude and action that you want Jesus to change in your life so you can better demonstrate Christ's love in your home.

_____

➤ Write down the names of three friends who need to know Christ and what you want to pray for them every day.

Names   Requests

_____   _____

_____   _____

_____   _____

➤ Circle the friend you think is most ready to talk about Christ. Think of one special thing to do for that person this week.

_____

➤ Go over the *Jesus: No Equal* booklet with your friend. This booklet will help you discuss the Gospel with your friends.

I am not ashamed of the gospel, because it is the power of God for the salvation of everyone who believes: first for the Jew, then for the Gentile.

**Memory Verse:
Romans 1:16**

To Help You Communicate
A special booklet will help you communicate the Gospel to your friends. You can order the *Jesus: No Equal* booklet from Reach Out Youth Solutions.
• **www.reach-out.org**

19

How Do I Get Plugged In?

A log burns brightly as long as it stays in the fire. But when it is taken out of the fire, it smolders and burns out. Meeting together with other believers keeps us "on fire" for Christ.

I have yet to find one person who has a growing relationship with Jesus Christ who has not plugged into a healthy family of believers.

 That's why God designed the church the way He did. Describe in one word a picture of the church in these verses.

→ ❯ Romans 12:4-5 _____

→ ❯ Ephesians 2:19-21 _____

→ ❯ Ephesians 5:25-27 _____

When you meet regularly with other believers in the local church, the church helps you in certain ways and in other ways you help the church.

 Let Others Help You
You will soon discover that you can get to know Jesus better by learning from others who know Him. Other believers will encourage you and help you grow spiritually.

When you think of church what do you think? Check one or more of the following:

☐ I'm bored.

☐ I wish I were playing ball.

☐ I've never been.

☐ I enjoy it.

☐ I have to get dressed up.

☐ I have lots of friends there.

☐ I go through the motions.

☐ I go only on Easter and Christmas.

20

What do the following verses tell you about the importance of getting together with other believers?

- ➤ Ecclesiastes 4:9-10 _____

- ➤ 1 Thessalonians 5:11 _____

- ➤ Hebrews 10:24-25 _____

As you make friends with other Christians, at first you may feel uncomfortable. But they can strengthen your faith and help you grow.

Get involved in a church that:

- • expresses openly the desire to know Christ.

- • teaches you how to follow Jesus.

- • has a spiritually strong youth ministry.

- • takes a personal interest in your spiritual life.

Think of one way that the church can help you.

_____

Power Thought

The Church is not an organization, but an organism.

You Help Others
Believers are involved in each other's lives. You have the special privilege of helping others.

 Read Romans 12:9-16 and write down all the ways Christians are to relate to "one an-other."

_____   _____   _____

_____   _____   _____

_____   _____   _____

What do you have to give to help the church?

_____

_____

Helping unbelievers is a part of what the church does too. That's probably how you became a believer. Someone reached out to you.

Christians have discovered the key to life — knowing Jesus Christ. Other people are searching for meaning in life. So believers tell others about Jesus.

 What do the following verses tell you about how to help others know Christ?

22

➤ Matthew 4:19 _____

➤ Matthew 9:36-38 _____

➤ John 2:35-42 _____

To express the Good News of Jesus Christ to others is an awesome privilege. You can tell them how Christ has changed your life and how they can get to know Him too.

MOVING OUT

➤ Which group of believers would you like to join? _____

➤ Ask someone in that group to take you to their group this week. Who? _____

➤ Determine one way that group can help you. _____

➤ Decide one way you can help someone in that group. _____

➤ Invite one friend to go with you who doesn't know Christ. Who? _____

And let us consider how we may spur one another on toward love and good deeds. Let us not give up meeting together, as some are in the habit of doing, but let us encourage one another – and all the more as you see the Day approaching.

Memory Verse: Hebrews 10:24-25

What Happens When I Mess Up?

Now that you know Jesus Christ, what happens when you lose your temper, slap your little brother, yell at your mom, or something even worse? Will Jesus give up on you? What do you think? _____

 Let's see what happens when you mess up (commit what the Bible calls "sin"). Sin is like saying to God, "I'm going to handle this situation my way". That is your natural tendency. According to **Romans 3:10-11**, how has that attitude of sin affected your life?

_____

_____

 Now that you are a child of God, sin can break your fellowship with God, but not your relationship with Christ. Your relationship with Him can never be broken. What does **1 John 1:5-7** say about broken fellowship with God?

_____

_____

If you take your dad's car when he asks you not to, and drive it into a telephone pole, that causes tension with your dad. You still have a relationship with your dad (you are still his son or daughter), but the fellowship is temporarily broken. Any sin creates tension in your fellowship with God.

How Do I Confess?

All of us sinned before we became followers of Jesus. And all of us sin after we become believers too. The difference is that now our sins are taken care of because of what Jesus did on the cross. What can you do to restore your fellowship with God after you sin?

Read 1 John 1:9.

_____

What do you think it means to "confess"?

_____

Confession means agreeing with God that you are wrong and honestly wanting to change. You agree with God that "I'm doing it my way" in that particular area of your life. Then you say to Jesus, "I want to change and do it Your way."

To confess:

- > Agree with God that you are wrong.
- > Thank God that Jesus died for your specific sins on the cross.
- > Ask Jesus to take that sinful area of your life and change it.
- > Take steps to correct your sinful attitude or action.

Saying the words doesn't mean you have confessed. You must have an honest desire to turn away from that sin.

Power Thought

Christians aren't perfect, just forgiven.

What Does God Do?

What does God do when you confess your sins?

Read 1 John 1:9.

He does two things:
• God forgives you every time.
• God forgets your sin forever.

When you confess your sins, God cleans the slate and restores your fellowship with Him. It doesn't matter how big or small your sins are. When you confess, God forgives and forgets.

Why? **Read 1 Peter 2:24.**

You may ask, "But what if I don't feel forgiven?" Keep in mind that you trust God by your faith, not your feelings. Forgiveness works in the same way. God doesn't want you to feel guilty. If you have confessed your sins, you can be sure that God has forgiven you. Claim God's promise in 1 John 1:9 and keep on going and growing.

If we confess our sins, he is faithful and just and will forgive us our sins and purify us from all unrighteousness.

Memory Verse: 1 John 1:9

MOVING OUT

➤ What sins in your life do you need to confess to God right now? On a sheet of paper list all of them, no matter how big or small. Confess those sins to God one by one. Thank Jesus for dying on the cross for your specific sins. Claim His promise that He will cleanse and forgive you (1 John 1:9). Ask God to take each of those sinful areas of your life and change them.

➤ Throw away the sheet of paper as a symbol of God's cleansing and forgiveness.

GETTING STARTED SESSION 6

How Will My Life Change?

Someone has said, "The only constant in life is change!" Possibly at this point you are asking yourself, "How is knowing Jesus changing my life?" Express how you feel about your life changing. How has it changed already? What still needs to change?

_____

_____

_____

_____

God will continue to show you the answers to these questions as you spend time with Him. He can see your life as a whole. Because of that, the changes He makes will always be in your best interest. According to **John 10:10**, why is that true?

_____

_____

Inside Out
People often judge others by their outward appearances – how they look and act. But when a person accepts Jesus Christ, the changes begin on the inside, not the outside.

You are a new person on the inside, even though you look the same and perhaps feel and act the same. When you became a follower of Jesus, God didn't give you a list of rules and regulations – do's and don'ts. Many people think that Christianity involves following a long list of rules. But rules affect only your outward behavior.

Instead of rules, God gave you the Holy Spirit. Where does the Holy Spirit live?

Read 1 Corinthians 6:19.

Now you have the Spirit of Jesus Christ – the Holy Spirit – living in you. The Holy Spirit is the source of power that will change you from the inside out. You have the inner strength to live the way God wants you to live. How does the Holy Spirit change you?

Read Romans 8:9-11. _____

Spiritual Breathing
Physically, you have to breathe to stay alive and healthy. When you breathe, you exhale carbon dioxide and inhale life-giving oxygen. Spiritually, the same is true. When you breathe spiritually, you confess your sin and let the Holy Spirit fill and control your life.

Making Changes
You may think, "I could never change some things about me. I've been doing them too long." You're absolutely right. In your own power you can't change them. But you aren't limited to your own power anymore. If you ask the Holy Spirit to work in you, He will help you make

those difficult changes. Look at God's promise to you in **Matthew 19:26**. What does that promise mean to you?

_____

When the Holy Spirit lives inside of you, your old life is replaced. You don't have to live like the "old you" anymore.

Read Colossians 3:1-17 and answer the following questions:

What makes it possible for your life to change? (v. 1)

_____

What do you need to do to help change your life? (v. 2)

_____

What do you need to do with your old life? (v. 5)

_____

What things do you need to put aside? (vv. 5-9)

_____

What do you need to "put on"? (vv. 12-17)

_____

God's power can change anything in your life.

Power Thought

Read Galatians 5:22-23, then make a list of the qualities of Jesus that the Holy Spirit has placed inside of you. As you list them, thank God that you possess each one.

_____

_____

 ## MOVING OUT

➤ Identify one specific area in your life that you want Christ to change.

_____

➤ What specifically do you need to "put off" in that area this week? What do you need to "put on"?

_____

➤ Where does the power come from to "put off" and "put on"? _____

➤ During the next week, begin to practice spiritual breathing in that one problem area of your life. Confess every time you sin and release the Holy Spirit to take control of that problem. Be sensitive to cooperate with the Holy Spirit each time that problem comes to your mind. Record any changes that you experience this week, even little ones.

_____

_____

Do not get drunk on wine, which leads to debauchery. Instead, be filled with the Spirit.

Memory Verse: Ephesians 5:18

Moving On

Now that you have gotten started in your life with Jesus Christ, you need to keep on growing so you can know Him better and better. Get with a group of friends and go through *Following Jesus* in the *Moving Toward Maturity* series. Go through each book in the *Moving Toward Maturity* series, one after the other.

FOLLOWING JESUS builds a foundation for a strong relationship with Christ. It addresses establishing a relationship with Christ, finding God's purpose and unique plan for each student, loving God and others and discovering God's will.

SPENDING TIME ALONE WITH GOD helps students develop communication with Christ through a meaningful devotional life. Students discover how to have an intimate daily relationship with Jesus through Bible study, Scripture memory, praise and prayer.

MAKING JESUS LORD challenges students to obey Jesus and give Him control in the day-to-day issues that students face. They discover how the Father, Son and Holy Spirit can change their lives on issues such as sex, friendships, possessions, parents, attitudes and habits.

GIVING AWAY YOUR FAITH equips students to communicate Christ to their friends. Through building relationships, starting conversations about Christ, telling their story and the gospel story, students build confidence to verbally identify with Jesus.

INFLUENCING YOUR WORLD prepares students to become servant leaders in the church and at school. Students live out the challenge of seeing hurting people, giving of themselves, caring for people and making disciples.

TIME ALONE WITH GOD NOTEBOOK offers a practical guide for spending time alone with God and a 10-week supply of daily outlines to keep it going strong.

JESUS: NO EQUAL BOOKLET
This booklet helps you present the message of Jesus to your friends.

You can order these materials from Reach Out Youth Solutions by visiting us online at www.reach-out.org

How To Take A Friend Through Getting Started

Follow these steps to walk with a friend through *Getting Started*.

- Go through the *Jesus: No Equal* booklet. Make sure that your friend has received Jesus Christ.

- Tell him that you want to help him grow in his new relationship with Jesus. Read together Colossians 2:6-7. Use the illustration of a garden. "Suppose you have just planted a garden. What would happen if you never watered, weeded, or fertilized it? But with watering, weeding, and fertilizing, it will grow. The same is true in your relationship with Christ." Ask him if he will get with you once a week for the next six weeks to work through *Getting Started*. Tell him you will work on it together, but that it will take some work on his part.

- Show your friend the *Getting Started* book. Go over the six issues covered in the book (see What's Ahead). Tell him that this is what you will discuss. Set up a time and a place to meet. Remember to call beforehand to remind him.

Discussing the Sessions

To use *Getting Started* most effectively, a new believer needs to discuss what he learns with a more mature Christian. That's you! Talking about the Bible verses and answers will help your friend grow spiritually. These guidelines will help you get a new believer started:

Tell him what. Tell him the goal of the session and what he should know when he completes it.

Tell him why. Base your discussion on Scripture and on your experience with Christ.

Show him how. Use practical illustrations and tools to explain the concepts of the book. For example, show him what you do when you read the Bible and pray.

Get him started. Do the lessons with him. Meet with him to work on the lessons together. Make sure both of you do it separately before you meet to discuss it.

Keep him going. Don't assume that when your friend does one lesson he will do them all, or that when he does